Richard St. John Tyrwhitt

Free Field

Lyrics chiefly Descriptive

Richard St. John Tyrwhitt

Free Field
Lyrics chiefly Descriptive

ISBN/EAN: 9783744775496

Printed in Europe, USA, Canada, Australia, Japan

Cover: Foto ©Thomas Meinert / pixelio.de

More available books at **www.hansebooks.com**

EE FIELD

Lyrics

CHIEFLY DESCRIPTIVE

BY

R. St. JOHN TYRWHITT

CHRIST CHURCH, OXFORD

London
MACMILLAN AND CO.
AND NEW YORK
1888

All rights reserved

PREFACE

MANY of these verses have already appeared, in the *Cornhill* or other Magazines; and I am answerable for their reproduction in this volume, with some additions. It is, I know, unwise to publish verses at a late period of one's life, unless after special experiences. But I may repeat a plea made under slightly analogous circumstances: that the production is only a very little one indeed.

R. St. J. T.

CONTENTS

	PAGE
THE SYRIAN FLUTE	1
THE FORDS OF JORDAN	6
ARAB GRAVES IN REPHIDIM	12
THE WELLS OF MOSES	19
THE PASS OF THE WINDS (NUKB HOWY)	25
THE JEWS' WAILING-PLACE, JERUSALEM	31
GENNESARET, 1862	37
DOWN DALE	43
BENDEMERE STREAM	47
WHITSUN EVE, 1885	50
LENT	52
LITANY OF RAIN AND WATERS, 1879	56
HEAUTONTIMOROUMENOS	59
FORMOSISSIMUS ANNUS	63
TINY	65
GLORY OF MOTION	68

CONTENTS

	PAGE
PENELOPE ANN	72
TO MAY—AUTUMN	75
LETTER TO MAY—WINTER	78
OLD LOVES	81
UNKNOWN YET WELL-KNOWN	84
THE SHEYKH'S STORY	86
OUTWARD BOUND	89
A RETURN	92
MY TUTOR'S FUNERAL	94
A LAMENT	97
HIGH CRAVEN, 1887	99
BEWERLEY MOOR	102
IVY—EARLY	104
KENNST DU DAS LAND—LATE	106
THE DAUGHTER OF MYCERINUS	109
FROM THE HUNGARIAN OF COUNT PETROFY	112

THE SYRIAN FLUTE

(NEAR TELL EL KHADY, SOURCE OF JORDAN, 1862)

It was a Syrian afternoon
In April, sweet as English June;
And fast and free our company
    Rode o'er the steaming Huleh plain,
And underneath the ancient tree
    On the first Eastern slope, drew rein.

Swarth English faces two or three
Among black brows of Araby;
With some remains of white and red
    On Yorkshire maidens, burnt nut-brown.
So where our scanty meal was spread

THE SYRIAN FLUTE

By the broad oak we lighted down :
And girths were slack'd, and bits withdrawn,
And, halter'd on the narrow lawn,
    The willing horses grazed awhile.
Our feet were deep in flowers alway,
The young bees revelled in the may
With one long song of summer-day
    Upon the blooms of the old Isle.
Ah me ! the noontide hour of ease,
    The halt beloved of beasts and men :
How daintily the southern breeze
    Caressed us ever and again,
While here and there a bird did seem
    To sleep, and twitter all in dream ;
And still the hallowed new-born stream
    Spoke softly now and then.

*   *   *   *   *

Who may forget the earliest sight
Of Jordan breaking into light ?

How he wells forth, strong and tender
 With his joyous inner sound,
No foam-threaded streamlet slender,
 But all limpid and profound.
How his fig-trees, gnarled and olden
 Cast abroad their fanglike wood,
Thrusting off the sere-leaf golden
 With the emerald-bursting bud.
How his ancient willows hoary
 Wave and whiten night and morn :
How his oleanders' glory,
 Like rose-fringes of the morn,
 Glows all delicate carnation
Round each wayward-wandering bay,
 Drinking deep in emulation
  Of the myrtle and the may
  And the lilies and the deer:
  And the spiry Reed, that bare
  On Earth's most awful day,

As the dread Dark began to fall,
The sponge of vinegar and gall
Man's mocking pity, last and worst
Up to the lips that said, I thirst—
    So runs the careless stream away.

  *   *   *   *   *

A quaint and tender little sound
    Came softly on my pilgrim's dream:
'Twas sigh and murmur all around,
    And that strange note did seem
Just louder than the stream and breeze:
    It had a buzzing tuneful tone,
As if the Grandsire of all Bees
Did there disport and take his ease
    Making a small contented moan.
I looked, and there upon a stone,
    Like David or like Corydon,
Or most of all like sylvan Pan,
There sat a gaunt and shaggy man,

THE SYRIAN FLUTE

Who play'd the Syrian reed—
The flute two-handed, which his peers
Had bade discourse through all the years
Since Israel piped with pipes, to bring
   His exiled shepherd mourning home:
   Since Western herdmen rose to sing
   Unto the reed of Greece or Rome,
Since Arcady, since Sicily,
Since ilex, beech, and chestnut-tree
   Saw shepherd's life, heard pastoral lay:
     That which hath been, the same shall be.
   Old Jordan runs on ceaselessly
   And man accomplisheth his day.

THE FORDS OF JORDAN

(FEBRUARY 1862)

LIGHT down, and ease our hacks awhile
   On the bald mountain's herbless brow,
And watch our stubborn mules' long file
   Come tinkling on, so far below.
That dreamy sound of little bells,
   It makes us think of evening flocks
On Alpine meads and Cimbrian fells—
   Amid these burnt Judæan rocks
That clink and crumble 'neath our tread
Where shade is none from blinding beams
Nor sigh of wind nor voice of streams

But fierce embrace of sunshine seems
    To blight its loved Earth dead.

'Tis scarce a hundred steps and one
    Across this ridge of frost and fire,
Before the Eastern view be won;
    Stray on, and dally with desire,
    Then lift eyes, and behold,
Hewn out without hands, they rise
    All the crests of Abarim,
Whence the Prophet look'd of old
Back, o'er misery manifold,
Forward, on the Land, unrolled
    Beneath his wayworn eyes.
Quivering all in noontide blaze
    Abarim, long Abarim
Glows, with very brightness dim
Even as when the Seer looked back
O'er the mazed grave-marked track:

Over Edom, furnace-red
O'er a generation dead
  When he knew his march was stayed.
Fiends and angels watched and waited
As the undimmed eyes closed slowly
As the vast limbs withered wholly
  From their ancient strength unbated:
As into the Vale of Shade
Seeing, not seen, he passed away:
And none knoweth to this day
  Where the awful corpse is laid.

*   *   *   *   *

The Dead Sea salt in crystals hoar
  Hangs on our hair like acrid rime,
And we are gray, like many more,
  With bitterness and not with time.
Two hours of thirst before we reach
  Yon jungle dense, and scanty sward,
For many a mile, the only breach

Where Jordan's cliffs allow a ford.
Now, spurs of Sheffield, do our will,
   And, little Syrian barbs, be gay;
All morn we spared you on the hill;
   Now, o'er the level waste, away
     With your light stag-like bound.
So cross the plain, nor slacken speed;
And brush through Sodom-bush and reed
   And tearing thorn, and tamarisk harsh,
   Wild growth of wilderness and marsh,
     Cumbering the holy ground—
Reach Jordan's beetling brink, and mark
The winding trench deep-cloven and dark:
The narrow belt of living green,
The secret wave that whirls between:
Death's river; sudden, swift, unseen.
He is changed from his gay going:
   Could we know the arrowy stream,
Once, whose tender talk in flowing

Cast us softly into dream,
　Darkling now with fitful gleam
In his precipices' shade,
Like a half-drawn Persian blade
　Of black steel, darkly bright?
At his birth he went not so,
Swelling pure with Hermon's snow,
　But joyous leapt in light.
Must he fare to the Sad Sea,
Through waste places, even as we?
Yet he makes a little mirth
　Racing downwards evermore:
And the green things of sweet Earth
　Cling a little to his shore.
Even so it is, so let it be.
But strip, and try your strength with him.
　He is the type of that black wave
Wherein the mighty fail to swim,
　The likeness of the Grave.

Also his waters wash us free
From salt scurf of the Bitter Sea:
Stem his dark flood with shorten'd breath
And take the lesson as you may,
That the Baptismal stream of Death
Doth cleanse Earth's bitterness away.

ARAB GRAVES IN REPHIDIM

(WADY FEIRAN, DESERT OF SINAI, 1862)

BACK leaned he in his saddle high
    That swarthy wild man of the East,
With reckless grace and kindly pride,
    Across the sinewy wayward beast
Who knew his hand and watched his eye,
    And cared for him and none beside.
His face was like the beakèd kings
    Who look from lofty-carven cars,
Hewn shallow, where Euphrates' waves
    Reflect the broad Chaldean stars.
    So on his loftier camel he

ARAB GRAVES IN REPHIDIM

    Rode master of a few and free,
      As they were lords of many slaves.

A little while he bade us stay,
    And pointed with a lean brown hand
    Towards a level space of sand
A hundred yards beside the way.
There lay the gravestones of his race,
    Their feet to East, their heads to West,
    Houses of pilgrims' perfect rest,
They studded all the silent place ;—
So blinding-bright and all alone
It seemed, that desert-isle of sleep
Only that shadows sable-deep
    Lurked imp-like by each sparkling stone.

It might have been the resting-place
    Of those who felt the bitter sword
Of Joshua, and the foredoomed race
    Of the dread people of the Lord.

They who strove in wrath and need,
    Hagar's sons and Israel's seed;
Desert-worn and famine-grim
In the gates of Rephidim:
    Where the listed battle swayed,
    Granite walls o'er reddening sands,
    Rising tiers on tiers,
While the Prophet's arm upstayed
    All day long by priestly hands
    Bade prevail his toil-worn bands.
While Egyptian axes hewed
Through the tough mimosa-wood
    Of the Desert spears.

Ran the dancing rivulet red,
    Sighing to its sighing palms,
Yonder, in the Serbal shade
    In soft rushes, and clear calms?
Laid they down their Hebrew dead

In sweet Feiran's small green mead
  There to hold the land they won?
Or beyond the rocky portal
  Rest they in great honour here,
Reckless of the noonday sun,
  Of the dint of bow and spear,
March, and thirst, and famine mortal,
  Sleeping without fear?
They had seen the fire and cloud
Down as shuddering Sinai bowed;
  Ever in each awful ear,
All through Amalek's yells of onset,
  Rang the Voice exceeding loud.
Therefore no man slacked his hand,
And they strove from dawn to sunset;
  Till their dead or living band
In deep graves, or fruitful portion
  Rightfully possessed the land.

*   *   *   *   *

The hot day wears, the shadows grow
    Full lean and long upon our way;
        Lo, my rough camel waxes gay.
The voice of streams, the scent of grass
    Before him in the palmy pass,
        He knows, he feels them miles away.
One cut and cry is all the need,
    The sullen strength wakes into speed.
Out shoots the long lean neck; forth launches
    Each foreleg, like a shoulder-blow.
And the propelling greyhound-haunches
    Urge on his mighty trot below,
        And the beast goes as he can go.
His stride is silent as a dream,
    The dancing mirage reels around :
The yellow rocks and glittering ground
    Fly past me, racing like a stream.
The plain is past ; scarce ten yards wide
Yawns that strange gash in Serbal's side :

ARAB GRAVES IN REPHIDIM

The Feiran Gates flash by;
Gray weeds and brown begin to spring,
Rough tamarisk and mimosa fling
    Wild shade invitingly.
Nor does the camel's footfall drown
    The soft voice of that little rill
Through moss and marish trickling down
    Below the golden hill:
Nor yet the palm-leaves rustling, sweet
    As the light fall of Summer rain—
O tones that promise we shall meet
    By our own shepherd streams again!

There is a certain English tomb
    Where, if God will, I will be laid.
    There are sweet waters and deep shade,
And a small weather-beaten church
With lichen'd wall and ivied porch,
And all around faint roses bloom.

There winter storm and summer rain
    Fall various, like the tears of man.
Some, wild-blown drops of utter pain,
    Some, dews of waiting hope and faith ;
Seed sown in grief shall flower again,
    And the dead beauty of that grave
        Shall not be held of death.
There's many a realm and many a wave
    Between us now and our old Land.
    But were I lapped in Desert sand
Before the Mount, 'twere all the same.
Unto the earth the earth-worn frame,
    The spirit unto God who gave.

THE WELLS OF MOSES

(NEAR SUEZ)

He rushes down, his course is done,
    The Dynast of the Eastern day:
The giant hath rejoiced to run
    Yet sinks with willing speed away;
And the wrath he could not tame
    Mightier Beauty doth relieve;
And the whiteness of his flame
    Is toned to rose of Eve.
Like a king who rules apart
    With an even hand severe,
Who hath needed, sad at heart,

Quell all souls with force and fear—
So, all day, his face austere,
  Bade us look not on our Lord—
And he dimmed our veilèd eyes
  With the waving of his sword
Across the blinding skies.
Now, through the fringe of yon fair cloud
  He spreads out radiant hands to bless,
And with a farewell, soft and proud,
  Looks down upon our weariness:
And from this last sand-ridge behold
  Where, ghostlike on the Red Sea shore,
Our pallid tent shakes at its fold;
It may be where the Tribes of old
  Lay faint and travel-sore,
While Egypt strewed the golden sand
  Rider and horse, all o'er.
Above, slim changing shadows glide
  From wavy stems of pillar'd palm

That toss their plumage side by side,
    And join in rhythmic measure calm;
As Hebrew maidens on the strand
    Moved in the dance that Miriam led,
        And bade their timbrels echo wide
    Their antiphones above the dead
        Israel should see no more.
Wide shallow pools along the beach
    Fill with the smooth encroaching sea
        Like magic mirrors quickly spread:
And up a vision springs in each
    Of eastern mountains rosy-red
        Floating and quivering blushingly.
Emerald and blue, the western brine,
Brings to our feet the glorious line
    Of the long Mountain of the Free,
Then hath the Master's hand portrayed
All hues of light, all tones of shade;
    And to the waves and mountains given

THE WELLS OF MOSES

A space of calm without a breath:
A tranced rest of glorious death;
    A brilliance like the gates of Heaven.

*   *   *   *   *

The ruins sparkle white and fair
  At Suez, in the Western beam—
  Where hasty wreaths of railway steam
  Pant upwards in the delicate air,
    Half gray, half sunset-rosed—
Where barren foam meets barren sand
    And Commerce leaves her wrecks exposed
  'Twixt weary sea and weary land.
Thick-strewn, the camel's bones lie there,
  Outworn, with all its patient strength,
  The Desert-ship goes down at length:
And just below the high-sea mark
Lie ghastly ribs of many a bark
  That rests from warring with the main.
There East meets West, and old meets new

And iron England rushes through,
   Her camels waiting for her train;
The restless messenger, who glides
Up to the verge of Indian tides
   Which rise to woo the inland waves
      Through their long channel, slowly won
   With toil and death of suffering slaves
      From Necho to Napoleon.
Ah, Progress treads a narrow way
   As strait as Faith's, and marked with graves.
With fiery speed and sick delay:
With sloth compelled, and feverish haste
Uncomforted, across the Waste
   Which man may pass, but never tame.
   He turns not from his deadly game:
   He toils from sea to boundless sea:
   He prays to rest where he would be:
He leaves the sand-trace called a Name.

*   *   *   *   *

But the long shadows stretch no more:
    A lightless flame of gold and rose
    Up to the crystal zenith glows;
The After-glow, when sunset's o'er.
    And hark, our tent-ropes, strained and strong
        Moan wrestling with the evening wind,
    Which now takes up its Southern song,
    And filling English sails unfurled
    Up from their Indian underworld
        Doth haste our Homeward-bound.
O gallant wind, O loving sound!
Spread carpet by the haunted well
Named of the Guide of Israel;
    Sleep dreamless sleep of wayworn men.
    To-morrow, sun and speed again;
    And many a march on holy ground.

THE PASS OF THE WINDS (NUKB HOWY)

(FIRST VIEW OF SINAI)

There is a swarthy fig-tree springs,
All in a weird convulsive form,
Half up the purple Pass of Storm,
With painful branches deathly old,
Her talon-roots take stubborn hold,
Like Spider in the house of Kings.
Yet her sad presence comforteth,
Her growth is stronger than the death
Of the pale granite which she cleaves;
Even to yon secret brooklet's brink,
Whence her far-seeking fibres drink
The life of her broad leaves.

O Camels of uneven mind,[1]
   We will not add another wrong
   To swell that growling undersong
Of many miseries undefined,
   Which it delights you to prolong,
   And ye shall scale this broken stair
   With lightened loads and saddles bare.
     Although ye murmur and rebel
     Like weary ones of Israel;
     As if those sullen souls who fell
Had made you heirs of their distress,
   And bade you, all your dismal day,
   Go murmuring through the Wilderness:
     And die, like them, beside the way.

O utter silence of the Waste.
   O death—bare giant bones of Earth—
For ever scarred, yet not defaced

---

[1] "Iniquæ mentis asellus."—HOR.

THE PASS OF THE WINDS

By centuries of frost and fire—
    Your ruin-throes give Beauty birth
In purple cleft and rosy spire.
Ye flush not with the changing green
    Of Northern mountains that we know:
Glorious and grim, the lifeless scene
    Reels wavering in its mirage-glow,
All sultry sheen and tender hue.
Up-rushing cliffs crystalline-red
Close in the path, and frown o'erhead
    Most like a flayed Glencoe.
They smile not here, March-flowerets new,
    They sigh not here, the Baptist's bees,
Nor know the taste of honey dew;
Their Desert-table is not spread
    With willow, myrrh, and tamarisk-trees,
As where dark Jordan hurries through
    His sweet wave to the Bitter Sea's.

Their wounds become the warrior hills
    Enduring all without a sigh.
Their gashes yawn, their thirst is sore :
    Theirs is no joy of tinkling rills
        All hurrying down delightedly
To join their central torrent's roar ;
    That strains and thunders to the sea,
    Most like a people fierce and free,
Who brook the curb and rein no more
For wrath that masters ruth and dread.
Here, but one tender-trickling thread
    Goes by like good men's lives unseen,
With stunted palm and fig-tree green,
    And blessing without word.
But hours and leagues have slowly pass'd
The Eastern ridge is near, at last—
    Climb onward, awed and spurred.
The desert-heats lie far below,
And see, a trace of lingering snow.

Lo, we have toiled, and we attain.

 Look down awhile with open heart,
Bid wrangle of denial vain
 A little hour to stand apart.
Think, here, at least it well may be
That Israel's leader stood to see
His trembling tribes roll countless by,
 To crowd yon miles of terraced plain
And cluster round with awful eye
 Before the Rostrum of the scene,
  Which mountains circle as a throne;
Whence leagues of sloping space between
 Rise softly to our camels' feet;
Where all the Race might stand like one,
Beneath the mountain and the cloud
And hear the voice exceeding loud
 Deal each a summons of his own
  Whither Israel, wave on wave,
  Entered in, expectant, solemn,

Every desert-wearied column :
Onward, with an even flow,
Up the sandy Debbet wide
In a dark and living tide.
Awed; forgetful for awhile
Of the living green of Nile,
Of the bondage left in haste
With its luxury and its rod.
Changed—for free winds of the waste
And the leading of their God.
Till their black tents, side by side
Made the granite and the green
Swarming-dark alike below :
Till the fiery Cloud stooped down
Deepening Sinai's cloven frown ;
Red, with dreadful light illumed :
Till the Voice and Vision came
Downward-rushing all on flame,
On the people loved and doomed.

THE JEWS' WAILING-PLACE, JERUSALEM

Sharp clash the hoofs on marbles worn
    In Sion's ruin-paven street:
Spare our tired horses' floundering feet,
    Light down, I tread the ways forlorn,
Where all seems canker'd with disease:
    If there be houses tainted still
    With scurf and scale of human ill,
They needs must crumble down like these.
And leprous men beside the way
    On whom the ancient Curse is laid,
Crouch featureless in cruel day
    And dumb and darkling sign for aid.
Cast down your alms, and hasten on

THE JEWS' WAILING-PLACE

    Foot-deep in Sion's festering dust,
    By close barr'd hovels, which incrust
    The walls, once marble rose—and white
Which Herod built—or Solomon.
Go down with yonder abject few
    In caftan green, or dim white veil,
Who hurry past to raise anew
    Their feeble voice of ancient wail
    Before Moriah's stones of might.
Scant beards are torn: old eyelids stream
    With many a sad unhelpful tear.
Man's weeping and earth's ruin seem
    To find their common centre here.
And scarcely more hath Time's decay
    Fretted the corner-stones on high
Than kissing lips have worn away
    The strong foundation's masonry.

    The Wise King stood on Sion ridge

THE JEWS' WAILING-PLACE

With purpled priests and chiefs in mail,
Where Temple-wards his soaring bridge
    Aerial, massive, spanned the vale.
Day and night his awful eyes
Gazed into all mysteries,
Night and day his voice was heard
Touching man and beast and bird
And all growing things that be
Towering-great or subtly-small;
From the red-armed cedar-tree
To the hyssop on the wall.
Did it vex his heart to know
How that sad mean herb would grow
Over every polished square
His high word had order'd there?
It springs—austere and pale and faint;
    No dancing showers, like fairies' feet,
      Bring feathered fern, and wallflower sweet,
And ivy-nets and mosses quaint

That deck decay in Northern lands,
Here spiny weeds grow harsh and gray:
Even as they grew, that Paschal day,
   When they were plucked by mocking hands
To crown the Victim led away.
—There mourn the sons, whose sires bade slay.

*   *   *   *   *

Well, we are modern ruins too
With back-turn'd looks to woeful when;
Yet can be keen as hounds at view
For work, or sport, or strife of men,
   Grief crushes not when strength is left.
O City of all sorrows, we
Forget our transient pains in thee;
   Seeing much abides, tho' more be reft.
The fountains of our eyes are dry
   With care and labour all the years:
But this we care not to deny,
   That, be they shed by girls or boys

THE JEWS' WAILING-PLACE

For love or pain, or broken toys,
Even idle tears—are always tears.
Why should our wayward souls refuse
    To sever scorn from sympathy?
One cannot weep with wailing Jews.
They howl, as toothless wolves may cry:
    They chatter like the autumn crane—
Each stands, himself a prophecy
    And moans his psalm, its hope unknown,
    While the salt drops flow on in vain.
Ah me! poor slaves whom none will buy,
    Sad thralls whom none will own!
Tears we have none—with awe and sighs
    We own, that these mad mourners' woe
Strikes hard on one deep-sounding chord.
    That the bright Temple lieth low,
Where, in the ancient centuries
    Men saw the great Light of the Lord:
Where eyes of flesh in latter days

Beheld the Saviour come and go ;
    A wide world's Light of softer rays.

*   *   *   *   *

What hope? the helpless thought intrudes :
    Pass the near postern : mount and ride
Where Hinnom's vultures wheel and feast.
Look North and South and West and East
    On silent Ophel's populous side.
There rest for furlongs far and wide,
    In shallow soil or rock-hewn cell,
The multitudes, the multitudes.
    And there is peace for Israel.

GENNESARET, 1862

Behold, the Waster's peace is here
    Dead silence after battle-bray.
Unlike the western spring-time dear,
    When English fields are hushed in May,
With populous calm of tender sound
    Of leaf and insect, fold and herd,
And wild birds revelling all around :
    Here sickly Nature hath no word :
The stubborn World's Debate is still
    In desolate rest, even since that day
When up yon western horned hill [1]
    The long day's strife did roll and roar,
Till broke the Christian arm and sword,

[1] Kurûn Hattîn (Saladin's victory).

  And their faint few might strike no more
The controversy of the Lord
His mindful mountains hear, until
  Their ancient strength shall melt away.

Thine is the quiet of the Dead;
  Yet hast thou known another scene,
What time the words of Peace were said
  Between thy peaks, Kurûn Hattin;
    When He in whom we live
Blessed those who love, spare, toil, forgive—
  All Earth's unknowing race in turn.
It may not fail, it hath not passed,
It holds for aye, from first to last,
That amplest blessing spoken then
On all the sighing sons of men,
  "Blessed are they who mourn."

He shall not reign, His people cried,
  They have their will, He holds His hand.

And still the Turkish scourge is plied,
  The wasting curse of man and beast;
And Desert tribes, like Desert sand,
  All the fierce children of the East,
    Go up like locusts on the land.

*   *   *   *   *

But yester-eve we lingered late
  (Being somewhat worn with sun and speed)
To watch, beneath Tiberias' gate
  The wild Hawâra play jereed.
Like swallow wheel'd each wiry steed,
Until the thief who him bestrode
  Deck'd with all colours of the Mede,
  Looked winged and birdlike in his selle
    So lithe and light he rode.
Beside the crumbling battlement
  (Shaken, the day when Safed fell
  In one wide carnage, earthquake rent),
The women gazed, and sang by turns.

They held their Bairam feast that day
    With mimic war and sport of love
    And whispering waved the palms, above
Volcanic fire that heaves and burns.

   *   *   *   *   *

The lovely lake fills up the caves
    That once were as the mouth of Hell.
The flowers laugh careless over graves:
    And tho' we mourn that Beauty dies,
    She hath her day—and it is well.
    A little time she flies,
All marred and weeping, like Love's Queen
From Diomedes' spearhead keen and gray;
    But ever again, where she hath been
Constant, not changeless, day by day,
    She triumphs o'er the scene.
As with the breathing of God's breath
    So dies she ever and is born,
    Hers are the gates of night and morn

Whence she doth marshal clouds and light
    In hues of glory manifold
From crimson wild to burning gold,
    To flame o'er fair things and forlorn
Though smoke of commerce dim the sun
    And din of trade offend the skies,
And all the pleasant streams that run
    Be clogged with mills and foul with dyes—
Yet falls the night, and morn doth rise
    In glory over all things mean,
And in the brightness of thine eyes
    Decay grows dear and darkness bright,
        O Mistress, O our Queen!
The broad white stars obey thy hand
    That wheel across the Arctic night
And o'er the savage northern sea
The night-long sunset glows for thee
    In nameless hues of unthought sheen.

*   *   *   *   *

GENNESARET

Feel bit and rein, draw girths, and mount:
   Yet gaze along the silent shore
Ere this delight shall join th' account
   Of all that we shall see no more.
The still lake mirrors slope and cliff
   Each standing o'er its shade, as if
The "Peace, be still" were lately said.
   The rosy oleanders glow
For miles of marge—a light of snow
   Rests on the northern waves, below
     Old Hermon's triple head:
   Only in dreams, beloved Sea,
   Our souls shall henceforth walk by thee.

DOWN DALE

(WHARFEDALE, YORKSHIRE)

From the shallow above the linn
That swallows wild Wharfe in,
An old cock-heron, with a sable tuft in his breast of gray—
With a fierce affrighted scream,
Like one, half-slain in dream,
Who wakes to Danger nigh
With armed hand on high—
So he cast him on the air, wild-flapping and all astray.
But a spiral sweep he made:
His beak, like a rapier-blade
At the guard he bore

His breast before,
And he took the wind in his wings, down dale he whirled away.

Heaped clouds on the moors to Nor'ad
Where their wrath had been outpoured,
And had streamed and flashed and roared half a summer's day :
By the lull'd wind gently driven
By the slant rays softly riven,
Touched with the coming of even,
Rosy like houses of heaven.
Solemnly pure and sweet, like Clouds of the Attic play—
With a maiden movement slow,
Gliding and bending low,
Sidelong by hollow and brae,[1]
A chorus in measure and rhythm, down dale they swept away.

[1] Διὰ τῶν κοίλων καὶ τῶν δασέων
αὗται πλάγιαι.—Aristoph. *Nubes*

But louder hour by hour
Waxed the river's voice of power:
Swoln from the sodden moor, and thundering pale or red;
Red in the depths of his might,
Pale in his wrath of fight
With the twisted dens and caves
That cramped his writhing waves.
(And you heard their boulders pounding helpless down his
whinstone bed :)
There were sills and doors of a home,
A dead sheep glanced through the foam :—
And whirling all without stay
Down dale he reeled, and he roared, and he raced away.

Yet through the dripping brake,
Where the torrent lashed like a snake,
Came one, by the fly-fisher's path, and the sounding shore—
Lonely, if not forlorn,
Grizzled, and tanned, and worn,

And old he seemed; but he sped
With a light-foot hunter's tread
On the rocks of the swirling stream that should know his step no more.
He looked to river and hill;
"Ye may gloom and brighten still,
When I am gone to the rest
Who are called and chosen and blest:
And I take up my word, and say
From the rise to the set of my day
He hath done well:" and his grave lips moved as he strode away.

BENDEMERE STREAM

CHERWELL (1883-4)

BENDEMERE Stream flows far away,
   Though it ripples close in an eldern ear;
There it is always westering day,
   There the summer is deep and clear.
   Feverish Youth, he comes not near.
"Elderly gentlemen" love to dream
"Sitting by side of this murmuring stream"
     Which sings as it flows
     By willow and rose
Over all things lost, and dead, and dear.

Whispering reed and wandering rose
    Iris and pale myosotis flowers
Sigh their scent—and the aspen throws
    Shadow and sound of tender showers;
    But there it never rains nor pours:
Still it is summer, laden and late,
Spellbound air hath slumbrous weight;
    And indolent bees
    Drone much at ease;
And fail to improve the shining hours.

The rose is faint, the rose-leaves fall;
    They drift like tinted scented snow:
    Still as the light airs come and go
The full-blown flowers droop, one and all;
    The Summer hath stilled the sweet birds' call:
    Creeping on with sun and moon
    The Shadow of Death, it chills the noon:
Sit by the stream, like Horace's clown:

At the set time it shall bear thee down.

    Thou must depart ;

    Lift up thine heart ;

Hope thy hope, and pray thy prayer.

WHITSUN EVE, 1885

(FIRST SPRING RAIN, OXFORD)

On bitter Spring's unlovely hours,
On frosted fruits and blighted flowers,
On parching hill and cracking plain
It comes at last, the southern rain.

The slow unwilling patterings seem
To gather to a tuneful stream;
The young leaves fall into the strain
And drip their drops of southern rain.

O living stream and blessing breath,
As life were with us, and not death :

WHITSUN EVE

All swelling buds are bursting fain
Wide open'd to the southern rain.

I am a broken branch and old,
My thought is dull, my heart is cold;
A breath of Thine on heart and brain,
O Lord, shall bless like southern rain.

Come Thou; it is the Whitsun Eve.
All earth shall joy, all flesh believe.
Possess all weary souls again,
Like piercing fire—like melting rain.

LENT

"For lo, the Lord is come out of His place."

    Up, my Soul, for this is He,
    Lo, He is come to see
    The wide world's iniquity,
        And all souls therein.
    Every crime and every woe
    He knoweth and will know.
    Bend, lofty head or low
Ch.   Because of thy sin.

    Turn thee from pain and toil,
    Leave thought of strife and spoil,

LENT

Draw thee out of dull turmoil
 And sick world's din;
Doff cloak and veil thou must,
Cast off Pride and Fear and Lust,
Cleave no longer to the dust
Ch. Because of thy sin.

Many brethren round thee press,
Little ones He deigns to bless,
Kneeling in great lowliness
 They shall seek and win.
Each is one, and thou art one,
Each answers deeds his own,
Each arraigned alike alone
Ch. Because of his sin.

O sad soul, hast thou fear?
Verily He dwelleth near;
Is it in great wrath severe

That He doth begin:
Pointing to the spear-wound red
In the Side thou hast pierced,
Lifting up the Hand that bled[1]
Ch.   Because of thy sin?

Wherefore hath He bowed His head
Down from high heaven
Where Time is vanished,
Where Space is riven?
From the crystal without shore,
Where thought can think no more
Wondrously He hath past o'er:
Ch.   Because of thy sin.

Wherefore hath He borne the weight
Of all toil and pain,
Humbled under death and fate

[1] See Ruskin, *Val d'Arno*, p. 194, on Orcagna.

LENT

      Chained with our chain?
From the hour thy sin began
Ripened on his awful Plan,
Even unto death, O man
Ch.   He hath borne thy sin.

Look, believe, rejoice to see
      He hath tender eyes for thee
And His red blood cleanseth free
      Outward and within:
He hath bled and wept and sighed
Are thine eyes so deadly dried?
Ch. full. O Loved one, hath not God died
      Because of thy sin?

LITANY OF RAIN AND WATERS, 1879

Lord, Thy Face is hid away
    In the cloud-dark of Thy Throne
And Thy mourning people pray
    All as one, and each alone,
Each with sins and cares to tell
    Many souls with one accord—
Lord, Thou doest all things well,
    Spare Thy people, O our Lord.

All the reapers mourn afraid
    Over wasted plain and hill,
Since Thine anger is not stayed
    And Thy hand is stretched out still

LITANY OF RAIN AND WATERS

Shall Thy curse of famine fell
    On Thy sheep be all outpoured?
Lord, Thou doest all things well,
    Spare Thy people, O our Lord.

Mirth is gone from out the land,
    Prayer and toil are all in vain
For the tempest of Thine hand
    And the plague of Thy great rain.
Give our weary souls to tell
    Of the sure hope of Thy word;—
Since Thou doest all things well,
    Spare Thy people, O our Lord.

And if long days we must pine
    Under stroke of this Thy rod;
It is Thou, and we are Thine,
    Be this all our thought, O God.
Strengthen against Death and Hell

All weak souls beneath Thy sword,
Since Thou doest all things well,
    Spare Thy people, O our God.

Let us know Thy coming Form
    While we strive with this rough sea:
Through the gloomy rack of storm:
    We are Thine, and we have Thee.
Dying or living, let us swell
    The one voice of Thy restored.
Lord, Thou doest all things well,
    Spare Thy people, O our Lord.

HEAUTONTIMOROUMENOS

Lo, at length thou art alone
    In a quiet room by night.
For an hour thy soul's thine own,
    Thou hast warmth and rest and light.
Rest thee, heart they will not read,
    Lay it by, thy mail of need;
Let all stabs and scratches bleed
    Till their aching pass away.

Hast thou cast down righteous seed
    Sorrowing, on the doubtful way

On to where all shadows lead
    Darkening to the full death-gray?
Thou hast sinned, and sinned again.
Therefore take home all the pain,
Every curious pang that flies
From foul lips and haggard eyes
    Cursing thy weak help in need.
        Let all bleed, let all bleed
        Till the smart be past away.

Did they prove thy coat of mail?
    Yes, they stung home heartily,
Yet thy heart did not quite fail
    And they drew no curse nor cry;
And they meant thee no great ill:
Not knowing thine, or their own will:
Could'st thou tell them all thy mind
They would sorrow and be kind,
Say no word and take no heed,

Let all bleed, let all bleed,
    All will bleed away.

Grows it slack, thy cord of fate?
    Does thy well-wheel creaking roll?
Hath the grasshopper his weight
    On the faintness of thy soul?
Are thy heaving sides well torn
With the rowel and the thorn,
Like the flanks of a spent steed
    That hath worn out the long day?
Stand thou still awhile, and bleed,
    Let all bleed away.

Thou hast fallen, and yet must fall
    Many a time beside to-day.
For thou art not wise at all;
    Verily, 'tis as they say.
And they err not, scorning thee,

Since even now they cannot see
    All thou know'st, of sin and need;
Sit thee down, breathe thoughtful breath;
Thou must smart, but not to death.
    Thou must work and bleed
    Yet awhile—for many a day.

FORMOSISSIMUS ANNUS

(OCTOBER 1884)

(WYTHAM WOODS)

THEY have done with the beans, they have carried the corn:
The white Autumn furrows are glittering and shorn:
The seven-o'clock sunshine is cloudless and clear
And sweet is the wane of the Beautiful Year.

The Port-Meadow turf echoes low as we ride;
And gay is the gallop by Isis her side:
Where float on still waters, more scarlet than sere,
The first-fallen leaves of the Beautiful Year.

Black rooks and gray starlings are mustering on high;
The blue herons wing over, with desolate cry,

The lapwings they whistle and wail far and near,
Are they sad for the wane of the Beautiful Year?.

Not they—nor we either :—in Wytham once more
The O. B. are out, with a stout cub before :
Push up the long hill into cover, and hear
Their earliest chime in the Beautiful Year.

Sweet birds and light leaves—ye may glitter and fly,
We send a sigh after, but only a sigh.
Thy death has a beauty that casteth out fear
With hope in thine ending, O Beautiful Year.

TINY

He met me in the street
    Half starved, with mangy fur.
With eyes and tail he did entreat;
    —He was a little cur.

I took him home, in short,
    Where in about an hour
Unto my wife he made his court
    And rose to social power.

He rather cut me then
    And ladies did pursue,
Finding them pleasanter than men
    I always thought so too.

In other dogs' discourse
    He likewise took delight,
To barking he had large recourse
    But never tried to bite.

From fat he fell to lean,
    Being old and sick: and then
He was the little dog he'd been,
    And took to me again.

I carried him to bed
    Sometimes—he was so weak;
He leaned a tiny worn-out head
    So soft against my cheek.

His death provoked no weeps,
    Nor any kind of stir:
But yet he seemed to reach one's deeps—
    That little dying cur.

Nor care I one bad word
  For parties far or near
Who may consider it absurd
  That he was very dear.

GLORY OF MOTION

(S. OXFORDSHIRE, 1878)

Three twangs of the horn, and they're all out of cover!
    Must have yon old bullfinch, that's right in the way:
A rush, and a bound, and a crash, and I'm over;
    They're silent, and racing; and for'ad away!
Fly, Charley, my darling; away and we follow,
    There's no earth or cover for many a good mile;
We're winged with the flight of the stork and the swallow;
    The heart of the eagle is lent us awhile.

The pasture-land knows not of rough plough or harrow,
    The hoofs echo hollow and soft on the sward:

GLORY OF MOTION

The soul of the horses goes into our marrow,
    My saddle's the kingdom whereof I am lord.
All rolling and flowing beneath us like ocean
    Gray waves of the high ridge-and-furrow glide on :
And small flying fences in musical motion
    Before us, beneath us, behind us are gone.

O puissant of bone and of sinew availing,
    To speed through the glare of the long Desert hours :
My white-breasted camel, the meek and unfailing,
    That sighed not, like me, for the shades and the showers !
And bright little Barbs, with veracious pretences
    To blood of the Prophet's, and Solomon's sires—
You stride not the stride, and you fly not the fences,
    And all the wide Hejaz is nought to the Shires.

O gay gondolier ! from thy night-flitting shallop
    I've heard the soft pulses of oar and guitar :
But sweeter's the rhythmical rush of the gallop,

The "fire in the saddle," the flight of the star.
Old mare, my beloved—no stouter or faster
    Hath ever strode under a man at his need—
Be glad in the hand and embrace of thy master
    And pant to the passionate music of speed.

T'ard Beauty—how quickly, as onward she races,
    And "comes through her horses" in spite of my hold,
I catch the expression of jolly brown faces
    Of parties a-going it over the wold.
They mostly look anxiously glad to be in it,
    All hitting and holding, and bucketing past;
O pleasure of pleasures, from minute to minute
    The pace and the horses—may both of them last.

   *   *   *   *   *

Can there e'er be a thing to an elderly person
    So keen, so inspiring, so hard to forget,
So fully adapted to break into verse on
    As this—that the steel isn't out of him yet?

That flying speed tickles one's brain with a feather;
    That one's horse can restore one the days that are gone:
That, spite of gray winter and weariful weather,
    The blood and the pace carry on, carry on?

PENELOPE ANN

A LITTLE bay, low in the shoulder,
 And more for her work than a Show.
Her stature don't strike the beholder—
 Get up then—see how she can go.
You'll not want a longer or taller
 To carry your weight in the van,
But only don't ask why we call her
     Penelope Ann.

One glance at that backbone and quarter,
 Those legs ever slender and sound:
And then only think that we bought her
 To the tune of a mild forty pound!

PENELOPE ANN

So mighty and free in her action,
    So kind to the handling of man,
She has got a certain attraction
                  Penelope Ann.

Hark forward! they've crashed out of cover
    One torrent of canine delight:
Just show her her place—and you're over:
    And give her her head—and all right.
No reason to hustle or wallop,
    Just sit down, as still as you can—
She'll never drop that dogged gallop
                  Penelope Ann.

You may go the short road with that lady,
    The customer's way, very straight,
While the devious, the prudent, the shady
    Edge off to be squeezed in a gate:
Watch those little ears, cocked for daring,

Hear the snort of that nostril of tan,
You may let her have that without caring—
>> Penelope Ann.

Sire? Dam? Well, she's bound to have had 'em;
　Or else she could hardly be there.
I don't know her breeder from Adam:
　But he knew a good horse and mare.
They must have been boldest, and kindest,
　And stoutest, that ever bore man,
So go it; you won't be "behindest,"
>> Penelope Ann.

TO MAY—AUTUMN

There's now and then a red leaf flying,
    Tho' the birches are hardly growing sere,
In the pines there's a gentle Southern sighing
    And we revel in the strength of the year.
There are late roses lingering not fading,
    But all through the long sweet day
We weary for a long sweet maiden,
    And she—rejoices in the name of May.

It is autumn brown, and the heather
    All bronzed and purple with the sun,
Sends its strong birds of dark-red feather,
    To rattle up, and crow before the gun

TO MAY—AUTUMN

" Pereunt," like the hours, " et imputantur,"
 They get shot and counted all the day—
But O, in spite of all the sport we want her :
 We can't anyhow get on without our May.

She walks by a Southern river,
 Her feet are deep in Southern flowers.
She hears not the birches' scented shiver,
 Nor the honied whisper of the moors.
She gets on sadly well without us,
 But swallow, swallow, fly to her and say,
Tho' she may not condescend to think about us
 Were all of us a-dreaming over May.

What's that springs between the stream and heaven?
 Would you tell me now, O salmon newly run,
Have you pass'd along the sounding shores of Devon?
 And did you jump, and see the Lovely one?

You don't answer: fish are uncommunicative.

Let me put twenty yards of line your way:

Now show your pluck and enterprise, you caitiff,

And rise at me, as I would rise at May.

LETTER TO MAY—WINTER

It was a gentleman of Crete
  Or Calydon, it nowise matters.
He rode from many a woodland meet
  As madly as all classic hatters.
His name was Cephalus; and why
  No reason's given that I remember.
But he cried Aura! in July,
  And I call May! in white December.

December won't be wintry when
  Our frozen floods bear that new-comer.
Come, Beauty—brings us back, per train,

LETTER TO MAY—WINTER

    Thy rose and white of early summer.
O Outside Edge ! O failing strength,
    O aged frame that often fallest !
Won't all our vows bring back at length
    Our fairest—and perhaps our tallest ?

Why comes she not ? all Oxford swells
    Are full of cares and sad surmises,
Why tarries still our Belle of belles,
    Nor skates upon the ice of Isis ?
Why comes she not ? Vain Echo cries
    Insultingly, " because she doesn't,"
And Hope in wilful negation dies,
    And May is mayn't, and can't, and mustn't.

*   *   *   *   *

But now along the mournful High
    Snow-piled above the horses' " hockses,"
There crawls a solitary Fly
    Bearing no end of ladies' boxes.

Lo she is here! and if not peace

She carries hope for patient waiters.

She lights, and brings our souls release,

And all is gas, and all is gaiters![1]

[1] I presume that Nicholas Nickleby has not yet become a classic, and lost its readers. The gentleman next door in gray stockings can hardly be forgotten.—*Author.*

OLD LOVES

Dear boys, you look hard as she passes:
    And briefly the truth may be told,
That all men may see without glasses
    We're both of us awfully old.
Like most of our friends, we are bearing
    The chilly revenges of Time;
But the Bard sings away without caring,
    And warms to the dance of his rhyme.

The raven hair's grown like a starling
    That flows by her pale coral ear;
But O, the dark eyes of my darling
    Were never more deep or more dear.

We both shall burn down to our ashes
    And sink with the flames of the Past. .
But the wildfire will leap through her lashes:
    The black brows will arch to the last.

The Record is writ in wan waters
    Of all the Beloved who are fled.
And Beauty may mourn for her daughters
    Who bloomed, and were dear, and are dead.
Life's dithyramb faints and goes slowly :
    Earth's blessing is matched with her curse :
And high is our hope, but too holy
    For treatment in cantering verse.

Why write it then?   Well—'tis permitted
    To tell one's old love-story o'er.
One can't always beg to be pitied
    With nænias about Never More ;
And nocturns, and roundels, and amor-
    ous atheism sung into space,

Are not quite invariably grammar.
>Now, that is correct in this case.

One glows over Beauty in splendour,
>One melts over Beauty in tears:
>
But a witch, like her sister of Endor,
>Is Beauty that's grown into years,
>
Old Memory and Honour are mighty
>To call us like bees to our Queen:
>
So dear is our ex-Aphrodite,
>So evermore—what she has been.

UNKNOWN YET WELL-KNOWN

(BADAJOZ, 1813)

WE left the plunder of the town while yet the East was gray:
All in the dewy dreary dawn we sought them where they lay
High-piled in that accursed breach, each as he passed away:
By night 'twas like the mouth of Hell; strewn like its floor by day;
   And who was he, and what was he? they asked it all in vain—
   The bravest brave, the foremost fallen, the flower of English slain?

None knew his number or his name, there where he lay outspread,
Thrust underneath their spikes of steel, foremost of all the dead.
We buried him proudly where he fell; we made the less of moan
That no man knew the shattered face—his mother had not known.

And if you care for fame of men, think somewhat on his fall.
He hath no name to tell, he lies unknown beneath the wall.
He gave his life most willingly, where willing men were all.
It may be that before his Lord his need shall not be small.
   Man may not judge of his desert, and human praise were vain
   For him, the foremost, flower and chief of all the English slain.

THE SHEYKH'S STORY

(GIBBON)

FULL late the sharp alarm was cried!
    Our waning fires scarce gave a spark—
    The midnight grew so deadly dark
Men prayed for light on either side.
The Caliph had a score to ten
    And right among our tents they rode;
    But evermore the strife abode
    Where Ali's broad blade rose and fell.
As a brother greets a brother,
    As the dry ground takes the rain
    Willing, not to part again—
    So we rushed upon each other.

THE SHEYKH'S STORY

Hard heads crack'd, and high blood ran,
Down went many a mailed man,
  Deep and choice drank Earth our mother!
But still Ali's strong hand swung
All those hours of swaying fight,
  Still the Loved One's voice low-thunder'd
  (With the words he never said,
  But he fell'd his foeman dead)
All night long, and time, two hundred—
  God is great, and giveth might!
So he smote without a frown,
So untouched he mowed them down.

*   *   *   *   *

I am Salam Ibn Seir,
  High Sheykh of the stout Rowalla.
All my chestnut beard and hair
  Have grown silvery since that day,
  And I've lived in chase and fray
Threescore years and ten—Mash Allah!

And, good youths, this is my rede:
In your wealth and in your need
All through life, and all through strife,
Do your best as we did then.
We loved Ali's hard-pressed men;
Ye shall hear your Lord's voice tolling
Over waves of combat rolling,
He shall cleave you out your way.

OUTWARD BOUND

(OCTOBER '83)

Ay, we were full, both heart and hand
    All those sore days of the sere leaf:
Untaught to pinch on English ground,
    They girded loins for the far land:
We kissed and clasp'd hands one last time
In that East-London gloom and grime.
For God had mingled wine of grief
      And that black cup went circling round.

Slow moved away the crowded train:
    Mighty it looked, soot-black and dread,
Uncouth and huge, in sight and sound.

It seemed as if a realm of pain
    Were claiming many hapless dead ;
Hapless, not hopeless, since they wept
For love and grief, and weeping kept
      To prayer confused, not wholly vain,
As that black cup went brimming round.

So many souls that single smart
    Of parting piercèd through and through ;
      So many felt the self-same wound.
So many a fainting sickening heart
    Felt keener grief and weightier
    And gave more weakly to the strain
      Because that others wept in vain :
And dulness had no wine and myrrh
      To slake that cup that circled round.

One poor old dame in those sad ranks
    Seemed overdressed, and fat, and plain ;

But Beauty's most becoming woe
    Had never touched one half so near :
For on the grimy Station planks
Her tears fell with the plash of rain
    Like blood-drops, audibly and slow :
And she nor knew nor cared at all
    What man or woman saw them fall.
And any journalistic swain
    Had pitied her, and spared to sneer.

"Now for the Shore"—and a great bell
    Dismissed us with its bullying loud—
To sooty train and squalid crowd ;
To thread the life-competing hell
    Of all that's worst in sight or sound :
    Through Poplar, to the Underground.
No more to do, no more to say ;
The cup was emptied for the day,
    Its bitterness had run the round.

A RETURN

Dear boy, at last you're home again,
    You're six feet one and twelve stone two,
And you can lead and dare and do.
    They call you valiant among men,
What else could come of you?
    Yet it seems rather sad and queer
To think you never again can be
    That little boy so very dear
Who really took my heart from me.

Grown out of knowledge—yes, 'tis sad,
    You are not what your mother knew,
The strong hard-bitten little lad

A RETURN

Who always had a loving look
And eyes as soft as dew—
>Yet could fight somewhat, and ride well
And was extremely hard to "sell,"
>And read, but didn't love his book,
And thought all pleasant tales were true.

Come home, if any home can be
Now she is gone and all is lost,
Come back again in withering frost
Who left us o'er the summer sea,
With glad up-anchor and away.
In whose long toil of work and play
Its joy seemed plenty for the day.
Well, hold that faith, nor count the cost,
Be glad and thankful while you may.

MY TUTOR'S FUNERAL

(EASTHAMPSTEAD, MAY 1883)

With its familiar clinking sound
    The Rectory gate behind me fell.
Some honied dews and scented snows
    From faint rich may, and guelder-rose
    Down-rustling, broke the silent spell
    Of that remembered ground.
Through masses of dark forest-green
    All brown and scarlet, brick and tile
The house stood rich and warm between,
    A pleasant place, a little while.

MY TUTOR'S FUNERAL

Sagaciously at ease they fed
   With dewlaps deep in summer grass
Those well-bred, well-contented kine :
   They raised no head, but let one pass
And never broke their social line ;
   The gray cob shook his head,
And fretted gently in his stall.
His friend the keen fox-terrier strayed
To find the hand he best obeyed,
   And listened for a silent call.

But all within was hushed and dark,
   And women wept, and men looked grim ;
And in a dread and darkened room
   Mine old best friend lay stiff and stark—
     I kissed the lips of him.
Had we known that, in strength and pride,
   When therefrom truth and learning came,

And Humour bicker'd forth like flame—
    Should we have laughed or sighed?

On the old study-table lay
    An empty album, which had held
Quaint photographs of many a friend,
    Far-fled and scattered, need-dispelled—
Priest, soldier, scholar—all away—
    Here, true love hath its end
And wanes like life, with moon and sun:
    Till the new Earth and the new Heaven
Hold all the choir of the forgiven,
    Till all be Love, and all be One.

A LAMENT

(AFTER WEBER)

RECKLESS birds are flying where my love is lying,
    There faint flowers are dying through the early fall.
Earth and Heaven shall keep her; nor may any weeper
    Touch that loving sleeper, wont to comfort all.
There shall earth lie lightly, there tall trees be sightly,
    There the moon look nightly, while the moon endures.
There let grow together fern and honied heather—
    For she always always loved the moors,

Under free winds' blowing, where the grouse are crowing,
    Better blooms are growing than all garden flowers:

Where the gray cloud hurries through the stony corries
    She and I did wander many summer hours.
She must lie and wither through the evil weather,
    And the Hope most holy comforts, hardly cures—
Yet o'er the Beloved plant the purple heather,
    For she always always loved the moors.

When the Lord erases tears from off all faces,
    Tears that left no traces, inner tears unshed,
Lo, we shall be changed—yet with tender graces
    Of their bygone beauty rise the faithful dead.
Love that never faileth is the same for ever,
    Man alone denieth; and the Word assures—
Meanwhile o'er the Dearest plant the purple heather
    For she always always loved the moors.

HIGH CRAVEN, 1887

WE drove by rocky dale and down,
    By Ribble side we caught the train.
We turned us to the hideous town—
    The autumn sky was gray with rain,
The mist hung low on Halton lea—
    And I was glad I could not see.

I could not see the warlock crest
    Of Pendle,[1] or the stream most dear,
Where she, the truest, bravest, best,
    Was happy with me, year by year,

[1] The Hill of the Lancashire Witches.

Until all ended on a day.
I was content to turn away.

Entered a squirearch's son or two
    And talked of gunning, grouse, all that :
How many a name and place I knew
    Came up through all their honest chat.
But the train batter'd at mine ear
And I was glad I could not hear.

*   *   *   *   *

Yet all was good, tho' all be lost :
    And joy was joy, tho' for an hour :
So walk no more, regretful Ghost,
    Round empty hall and broken bower.
He giveth rest and drieth tears,
Even drops unshed—kind are the years.

The thought and love, the fire and mirth,
    All pleasant things that made thee gay—

These are "thine ornaments" on Earth
  Thou needs must put them quite away:
Then, stand and wait, or rise and go,
"What to do with thee He will know."[1]

  [1] Exodus xxxiii. 5.

BEWERLEY MOOR

There's a slow moving mist on the breast of the hill,
The breath of the morning is touched with a chill;
The heather is reddened a bit in its tone,
And Autumn is glowing, but Summer is gone.

Full fair is the high sheltered garden of ours :
You may hear the grouse call, where you sit with your flowers;
All colours are changing, both evening and morn,
With a mellower beauty—but Summer is gone.

It's "tender," and "subtle," and "shimmering"—O dear!
We've come to the elderly stage of the year—

And O for the fire and the life of the sun!
One's heart rather fails one, when Summer is gone.

I'm greatly past forty; and therefore should "know
The worth of a lass," and I don't put it low;
I'm rather autumnal, and rather alone—
But I think of you still—tho' the Summer is gone.

IVY—EARLY

Thy shining head shall wear the wreath
    Which once the wild Bacchante bore,
Thy violet eyes shall shine beneath
    Brighter than all before.
All things lovely have their day,
    Fair and dear must pass away,
    Even the Ivy must decay
        With all bright heads that wore.

I know, and care not—care not thou :
    I swear what all mine elders swore,
O Darling, I believe thee now
    Lovelier than all before ;

As thy looks send back the light
  Like thine ivy dark and bright ;
  And thy deep eyes of pure night
    Rest, rest evermore.

Thine Ivy once shone glad and brave
  O'er wine-wet hair and wine-flushed brow.
Since—it hath deck'd full many a grave—
  They call it pensive now.
Yet thy crown it well may be,
  Since in sadness or in glee
  None may smile or sigh like thee,
    So wear thine ivy-bough.

KENNST DU DAS LAND—LATE

Know'st thou the land of golden morn
   All glare of heat and flame of light,
Where over perilous wastes forlorn
   The great sun rides in tameless might?
Ah me, to think of two short hours
In Feiran's palm and tamarisk bowers
   In that fresh islet of the sand
   Green with the green of our old Land;
With its one tender-trickling hill
And whispering palms woven overhead,
And granite peaks above, rose-red—
O dear lost Love, if that might be
There would I rest awhile by thee.

We knew the immemorial snow
    On silent ridge and savage Horn;
The silver summits far withdrawn
    The pale rage of their torrents' flow,
Their rosy peace at eve and morn
    Their power of storm, their still noon-glow.
The palm's no lovelier than the pine,
Nor, if my hand lay warm in thine,
    Which roof'd us, should we care, or know.
Lost love, although it may not be,
    My soul yet wanders there with thee.

We knew the red hills of the deer
    The glory of their purple heath,
The mirror of the breezeless mere
    The west wind's honey-laden breath,
The sturdy hunter-craft all day,
The crawl, the rush, the shot, the bay,
    The stout hart stretched upon the sward—

And thine the brightest eyes of all
To greet us home at evening fall,
    And thou my Queen, and I thy Lord—
Long hours and glad by moor and glen
Are gone with thee, nor turn again.

And now thou know'st the quiet shore,
    The region very far away,
The nightless rest for evermore,
    The Day that is not as one day—
Where faith is right and doubt is o'er
    And pain a nothing of the past,
Where God shall heal the heavy sore
    I must bear onward to the last:
And I shall look again on thee.
    Even so, lost love, so let it be.

THE DAUGHTER OF MYCERINUS

(HDT., ii.)

FASTEN back yon heavy-folded awning,
    Let me look upon the dying day:
I shall never see another dawning
    And in light I fain would pass away.
        Let the red sun shine
        Where his glance divine
    Yet may cheer mine unforsaken clay.

Raise me up, and turn my face to Northward
    Where old Nile runs turbidly and strong;
All day long I heard him sweeping forward
    And he seems to bear my soul along,

THE DAUGHTER OF MYCERINUS

  Strangely bearing me
  To an unknown sea,
All in measure to an inward song.

Come thou near me, father, call me Dearest.
 Other name thou never had'st for me;
Let me hear thee once again, thou cheerest
 This faint spirit, faint but nearly free,
  Let thy love again
  Stronger than all pain
Breathe upon my soul invincibly.

Take my hands in thine, and press them to thee.
 Lay thy cheek to mine, nor sorrow now:
For our gods' cold hatred doth pursue thee,
 Face their thankless anger—fear not thou,
  Not for any prayer
  Will our tyrants spare,
Not for mystic dance or frantic vow.

Thou art gentle, and their need is slaughter:
  They are strong to smite, and thou to save:
Thou art not as they are; and thy daughter
  Goes before thee to her maiden grave.
    Yon pale shallop waits
    And the cold-eyed Fates
  Beckon queen-like over that dead wave.

Father—while there yet remain that love me
  Yearly let them bring me from my rest,
Let the well-loved sunshine brood above me
  Tho' it wake no warmth within my breast.
    So my soul shall be
    Very near to thee,
  Seeking all on earth it loved the best.

FROM THE HUNGARIAN OF COUNT PETRÖFY

(KILLED IN ACTION 1869)

If that the Lord stood near and said,
"My son, I give thee power
To choose thy time of mortal dread,
And name thine own dark hour"—

So should it fall at Autumn tide,
In Autumn blithe and brown;
Ere winds be wild, or sere leaves piled
Before the winter's frown,
With one late-lingering bird to sing
In sunshine glinting down.

FROM THE HUNGARIAN OF COUNT PETRÖFY

I'd sing my last, as blithe and free
As birds among the may,
And up to heaven my voice should flee
And fair and brave should echo me
Until I passed away.

And when the charm hath left my lips
And when the song is o'er,
Come thou, my Heart, the flower of earth,
Come though thy soul be sore,
And shake thy tresses down like Night
And kiss my lips once more.

But if this be too good for man
God send my death in Spring,
When men be met on either hand
When maddening trumpets sing,
And stabs and blows bring out the Rose
From stout hearts blossoming.

Blow, trumpets—sing like nightingales,
    Make glad the swordsman's mood;
And so from out my heart of hearts
    Spring up, dark Rose of blood.
And as my right hand drops the sword
    My left forsakes the rein,
Come thou, O Freedom, deep-adored,
    Come glancing down amain,
And press thy fiery lips to mine
    That speak no word again.

THE END

Printed by R. & R. CLARK, *Edinburgh.*

BY THE SAME AUTHOR.

OUR SKETCHING CLUB.

LETTERS AND STUDIES ON LANDSCAPE ART.

WITH AN AUTHORISED REPRODUCTION OF THE LESSONS AND WOODCUTS IN

MR. JOHN RUSKIN'S

"ELEMENTS OF DRAWING."

Fourth Edition.   Crown 8vo.   7s. 6d.

"To persons learning to draw, the book cannot fail to be of immense service. For the general reader it has charms in the raciness of its style, in the pleasing pictures it affords of an interesting phase of English life and character, and in its graphic sketches of stirring adventure by the salmon river or on the hunting field."—*The Scotsman.*

"This pretty little book is half art manual, half novel of the usual kind, and all charming."—*The Literary Churchman.*

"We heartily recommend *Our Sketching Club* to anyone who wishes to learn to draw."—*Edinburgh Courant.*

"An excellent art manual."—*The Leeds Mercury.*

"Its pages are interesting, and containing many excellent and profitable suggestions."—*The Independent* (New York).

MACMILLAN AND CO., LONDON.

New Edition, revised.   8vo, half bound.   Price 18s.

A HANDBOOK OF PICTORIAL ART.

With coloured Illustrations, Photographs, and a Chapter on Perspective, by A. MACDONALD.

"A better and more useful handbook has never yet been published. We cordially recommend it to all who desire to possess the power of reproducing scenes which have given them delight, and of adding to the pleasure of all their friends."—*Birmingham Daily Gazette.*

"Past experience of Mr. Tyrwhitt's powers as an observer and a writer had led us to anticipate a good book on the subject of art, and we have not been disappointed. His work is not only well and pleasantly written, but full of useful information and valuable suggestions."—*Cambridge University Gazette.*

HENRY FROUDE, OXFORD UNIVERSITY PRESS, LONDON.

MESSRS. MACMILLAN AND CO.'S PUBLICATIONS.

Now Publishing. Vol. I., January 1888.

NEW EDITION OF LORD TENNYSON'S WORKS.

THE WORKS OF LORD TENNYSON. *LIBRARY EDITION.* A new and complete Edition in Eight Volumes. Globe 8vo, 5s. each. Each volume may be had separately, and they will be published in the following order:—

EARLY POEMS. Vol. I.	*January.*	ENOCH ARDEN: AND IN	
EARLY POEMS. Vol. II.	*February.*	MEMORIAM	*May.*
IDYLLS OF THE KING	*March.*	BALLADS: AND OTHER POEMS	*June.*
THE PRINCESS: AND		QUEEN MARY: AND HAROLD	*July.*
MAUD	*April.*	BECKET: AND OTHER PLAYS	*August.*

Poems by the Late Professor J. C. SHAIRP, Principal of St. Andrews. [*In the Press.*

A Volume of Poems by the Rev. STOPFORD A. BROOKE, M.A. Crown 8vo. [*In the Press.*

Mr. Matthew Arnold's Complete Poetical Works. New Edition, with additional Poems. Three vols. Crown 8vo. 7s. 6d. each. Vol. I. Early Poems, Narrative Poems, and Sonnets. Vol. II. Lyric and Elegiac Poems. Vol. III. Dramatic and Later Poems.

Charles Kingsley's Poems. Eversley Edition. 2 vols. Globe 8vo. 10s.—Popular Edition. 1 vol. Crown 8vo. 6s.

The Poems of Arthur Hugh Clough, sometime Fellow of Oriel College, Oxford. Eleventh Edition, with new Memoir. Globe 8vo. 6s.

BY GEORGE MEREDITH.

Poems and Lyrics of the Joy of Earth. Extra fcap. 8vo. 6s.

Ballads and Poems of Tragic Life. Crown 8vo. 6s.

BY CHRISTINA ROSSETTI.

Poems. Complete Edition. With Four Illustrations. Extra fcap. 8vo. 6s.

A Pageant, and other Poems. Extra fcap. 8vo. 6s.

English Poets. Selections, with Critical Introductions by various Writers, and a General Introduction by MATTHEW ARNOLD. Edited by T. H. WARD, M.A. 4 vols. Second Edition. Crown 8vo. 7s. 6d. each.

Vol. I. CHAUCER TO DONNE.	Vol. III. ADDISON TO BLAKE.
II. BEN JONSON TO DRYDEN.	IV. WORDSWORTH TO ROSSETTI.

MACMILLAN AND CO., LONDON.

www.ingramcontent.com/pod-product-compliance
Lightning Source LLC
Chambersburg PA
CBHW020127170426
43199CB00009B/678